One Key to Gender Balance

20-First Century Leadership

Avivah Wittenberg-Cox

BUILDING BALANCED BUSINESSES

© 2016

Published by 20-first Publishers

ISBN: 978-0-9935463-1-0

www.20-first.com

The world is changing...

(fast)

21st Century Shifts

Where the rise of women is one of
the four world-changing "W's"

Web
Technological revolution changes
how we make, buy and distribute...
everything.

Weather
Climate change forces adaptations
in sourcing, production and
distribution.

World
**Multi-polar world demands
multi-cultural mindsets and
understanding.**

Women
Massive arrival of women into
labour force and consumer base
creates huge new opportunities.

Companies need to broaden their vision to become more...

"gender bilingual"
as the world rebalances

Women are now most of the *talent...*

60%

of global graduates are now female

...and much of the *market*

80%

of consumer goods purchasing decisions are made by women

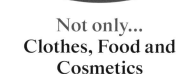

Not only...
**Clothes, Food and
Cosmetics**

But also...
**Technology, Real Estate,
Financial Services
and Cars**

Markets
The Common view

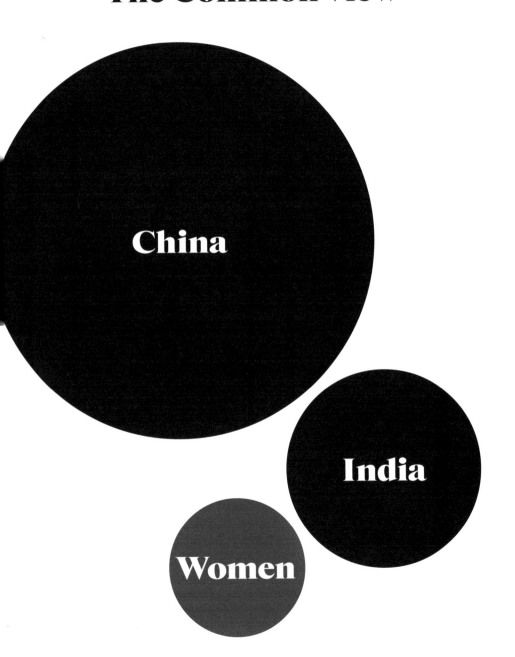

China

India

Women

Markets
The Reality

Women

China

India

Today

Gender Balance is not a nice to have...

It's
DO
or...

Where Are You

Gender Balance
is a Journey

A simple metric speaks volumes: the gender balance of a company's *Executive Committee.*

A pretty good measure of the priority companies have given the issue over the past 20 years.

Starting Smart
(1 woman in an
operational role)

Token
(1 woman in a
staff function)

(No balance. Exclusively male executive team)

Critical
mass
(25% minimum of
both genders)

Progressing
(15% minimum of
both genders)

(40% minimum of both genders)

But.

the problem is

(Pass it on)

Most traditional
approaches

DON'T
W RK

8

Mis-Framing the Agenda

With gender, it's how companies frame the issue that creates (or not) a culture of change.

The rise of women is like the rise of China. It is profoundly transformational, not just for the women (or the Chinese) involved. But for every country, company and couple on the planet.

1

HR issue
Nice to have
Socially good
Women in leadership
Diversity dimension
Led by women,
for women

Or

2

Strategic priority
Business issue
Stronger teams
Better insights
**Satisfied
customers**
Innovation
CEO-led
Management
accountability

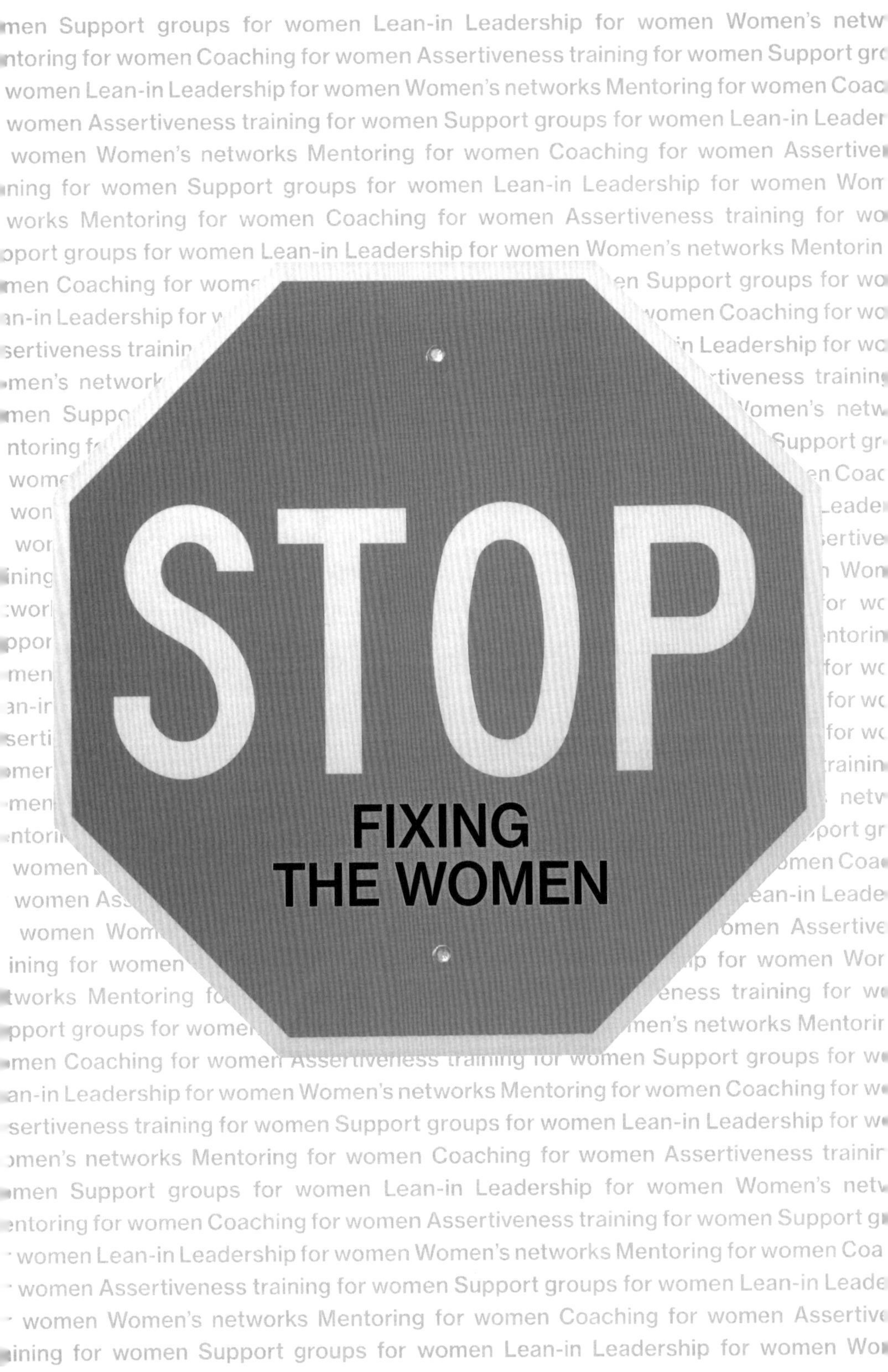
STOP
FIXING
THE WOMEN

Fixing the Women

Most companies think that the lack of gender balance in senior roles is a women's issue.

The underlying question behind almost all the work done in this space can be summarized as:

'What's the matter with women that they are not making it to the top? Let's help them...'

And 'help' them we have, for decades. The dominant approach to the lack of gender balance in most companies is to unleash a suite of 'fix the women' initiatives focused exclusively on women. Men appear only as 'champions', but are rarely in any way responsible or accountable for the imbalance that exists and persists.

The results, standing here in the early 21st century, have been underwhelming. Most companies and more managers are frustrated at the lack of progress. There is a lot of

gender fatigue

in companies that feel they have tried everything – and failed – to crack the issue.

Most haven't even really started yet.

Women as ~~'diversity'~~

Another mistake is putting gender under the diversity umbrella, referring to gender balance as a 'diversity' issue. Within companies' diversity efforts and many 'affinity groups' and 'employee networks', there is usually one aimed at women (despite the fact that women constitute 50 per cent of every other dimension of diversity). This is an effective way of keeping woman what they are not: one minority among many to be managed.

80%
Market

60%
Talent

This may have seemed logical in the 1980s, when women were actually a minority in the business world. But now that women have become the majority of the educated talent the world over and the majority of many companies' customers, is it logical to refer to them as a 'diversity' dimension at all?

They are your future.

Who is calling *who* diverse?

So....

Do your Leaders *get* it?

Do they buy it?

And can they sell it?

Are they Gender Bilingual?

Fluent in the language and cultures of both women and men?

Gender Bilingual

The management competency that equips all managers, male and female, to understand the differences between genders in order to be able to effectively recruit, retain and develop 100% of the talent pool, and to be able to understand, connect and communicate with 100% of customers, end-users and stakeholders.

Gender Balance

The balance of men and women that reflects the available talent pool for an organisation and sustainably supports its strategic objectives. As one CEO told us, "Not necessarily 50/50, but closer to 50/50 than to 85/15." Communicating that you are after 'balance' rather than 'promoting women into leadership' is one of the easiest ways we know to get the guys on-board. A small step in communications, a huge step in the perception of almost everyone.

Bilingual Marketing

Sales and marketing approaches that connect equally effectively with both male and female customers and end-users. An example would be the iphone, a bilingual product whose mass customer base is made up of men and women in equal measure. This in contrast to the 'pink' phones that telecoms operators produced for what they considered the 'women's segment.'

Gender Asbestos

A metaphor to describe the reality in most companies. The ratio of women relative to men begins to drop relatively early on in careers, creating a gender imbalance in senior management and leadership. This differs from the more commonly used term 'glass ceiling' which gives the impression that women only face obstacles at the top of organisations. This misperception affects the policies put into place to remedy it.

Critical Mass

The level at which any minority is no longer seen as one, usually considered to be somewhere around 30%. In companies, therefore, it is better to have at least 30% of either gender across all functions and levels, rather than having 80% women in staff functions and 80% men in operational roles.

Gender Neutrality

The ability to make all communications and policies inside organisations inclusive of all men and women, without focusing particularly on one gender or the other, which often creates a backlash. So, for example, replacing 'maternity' issues with 'parental' issues, and 'work/life balance for women' with 'flexibility for all'... In other words, allow men to be human too. The fastest way to get women into leadership is to enable men to have personal lives. Now, that would really be leveling the playing field.

There is only *one* key to

success

Leadership
Leadership
Leadership

(It's worth repeating)

Leadership
Leadership
Leadership

Have you prepared your Leaders, Culture and Systems for...

21st century *talent* and *markets?*

Simple Steps to Start

2
Shift the Culture: Focus on Your Majority

1
Recognise the Business Opportunity

Want to keep going?
Read:
*7 Steps to Leading a Gender
Balanced Business*

3
Get the Systems to Match

Just remember!

➡ **Make it a business imperative: all about customers, talent and opportunity**

➡ **Focus on leaders, not on women: equip them with the strategic understanding and management skills to work across genders**

GO ON

tap the benefits of balance...